119981

D1577064

DUFF HOUSE

A A Tait, MA, PhD

Professor of Art History, University of Glasgow

Edinburgh
Her Majesty's Stationery Office

A CLASSIC CASTLE

uff House, situated on the outskirts of Banff, was designed and built by William Adam for William uff—who was later to become the 1st Earl e. Work began in 1735 with an pressive design which matched Adam's ually grand work at Hopetoun House d Hamilton Palace. Unfortunately, merous problems arose which came to a ad in a financial dispute which stopped ork in 1741. Little work was carried out ring the developing legal wrangle which as only and finally settled in 1748, a few onths before William Adam's death. After the legal dispute, the 1st Earl lost terest in Duff House and the building as left incomplete and undecorated. owever, Lord Macduff, who succeeded s father as the 2nd Earl in 1763, was more thusiastic and made a determined effort finish the house and furnish it as grandly possible. Though he failed to build the dam wings, he did at least give the house s impressive interior. It was only in 1870 at David Bryce junior added one of the vo wings in a solidly classical style. onetheless, during the nineteenth ntury successive Earls Fife rarely spent ng periods at Duff House. Although the uilding played many roles, after 1940 it came increasingly neglected, ultimately mpty and in disrepair. It was acquired by e Ministry of Works in 1956, and is now

maintained for the benefit of the nation by the Scottish Development Department.

Although the house is no longer inhabited or furnished the visitor can envisage, with a little imagination, its past character. It served the succeeding Earls Fife as an administrative and social centre for their vast landed estates. Its contents—pictures, library and furniture—all supported the style of a highland nobleman in the eighteenth and nineteenth centuries. The house was arranged as a piece of social machinery with the basement—or ground floor—occupied by sparsely furnished servants' quarters, the pantry and the wine and ale cellars. From here the great external horseshoe stair, which can still be ascended, led to the first floor vestibule where important guests were received. The other rooms on this level mainly provided drawing room, dining room and bedroom accommodation for the owner and his family while on the floor above there were the principal reception rooms, the Salon and further bedrooms. The attic storey was to provide retreat and the gallery there a panoramic view over the Fife estates.

This guide-book places Duff House within the context of its park, but only the house is in the care of the Secretary of State for Scotland and open to the public.

William
Bráe

WILLIAM DUFF & WILLIAM ADAM

uff House was designed and built by William Adam for William Duff, Lord Braco and later 1st Earl ʼe, whose family belonged to a Highland tegory of the nouveaux riches. Lord aco's career and his entire way of inking were dominated by an ambition ɔt only to succeed but to be seen to have ɪccess. The mansion and surrounding tate at Duff House were as much part of ɪch a scheme of things as his ascent ɪrough the peerage—Lord Braco in 1735, ɪrl Fife in 1759. His son and successor, the 2nd Earl, completed such a cycle and so between 1735 and 1800 one of the great Highland estates was formed with Duff House as its capital.

Lord Braco's chosen path to wealth was as a dealer in land bonds, a lucrative area in Jacobite Scotland where 'money was scarce, land cheap, interest high, and rents low'. Acquired earlier in this fashion was the estate of Balvenie whose castle had a particular historical appeal for Lord Braco. Though ruinous, its possession symbolised success and gave its owner instant local

ɔposite. William Duff, Lord Braco, who commissioned ɪ building of Duff House in 1735. This painting is ither signed nor dated, but it has been attributed to ɛseph Highmore. (Reproduced by kind permission of ɪe Duke of Fife)

An eighteenth century engraving of Balvenie Castle showing also Balvenie House (right background), designed for William Duff by James Gibbs in 1724.
Balvenie Castle at Dufftown is in the care of the Secretary of State for Scotland and open to the public.
(Reproduced by kind permission of the Royal Commission on the Ancient and Historical Monuments of Scotland)

pectability if not nobility. It was at
venie that Lord Braco opened his true
eer as a builder and displayed a taste
ical of a Scotsman in the 1720s, heavy,
mal, dignified but with a sudden flash of
ost quirky individuality. His new
venie, designed for him by James Gibbs
Aberdeenshire born architect, reflected
autious sobriety in contrast with the
uberant vanity later displayed at Duff
use. Yet, whatever lessons Lord Braco
rnt in building Balvenie, they were
gely forgotten when he came to Duff
use.

William Adam received the commission
Duff House in May 1735. He had slowly
ended the ladder to architecture,
rting at the first rung as mason, then
d surveyor and improver, until
erging in the 1720s as an architect in his
n right. Duff House must have seemed
him as the just reward for such a
instaking apprenticeship. His design
lected this satisfaction for it was a
mination rather than any new
velopment in his practice. The complex
cade he proposed, the pattern-making
d sculptural decoration were all
ralleled in his earlier work at Hopetoun
ouse and Hamilton Palace on an equally
and scale. But at both Hopetoun and
amilton he was completing the work of
hers whereas at Duff House he was his
vn master. In all, he showed an
thusiasm for baroque classicism and
splayed at Duff House a masterly
ndling of the giant pilaster in a vertical
mposition. Such a baroque taste strongly
ntrasted with what is frequently accepted
his more modern manner—that of the
alladian villa—which is best seen at
rniston and The Drum, and on a larger
ale at Haddo in Aberdeenshire. But his
ans for both palace and villa, baroque or
alladian, were much the same variation of

the traditional arrangement of main block
and flanking pavilions.

The Start of Building

Work on the house started with
commendable speed, but in this haste were
rooted many troubles. No proper contract
was made between Lord Braco and William
Adam, no estimates of total cost given, no
proper system for hiring men or their
control, or of procuring the building
materials decided upon. Even the plan for
the house itself was far from complete. In
October of 1735, with the foundations laid,
Lord Braco wrote to William Adam
reflecting that 'the Design comprehended a
greater House than he had occasion for;
and therefore desired Mr Adam to reform
the Plan, and to abridge the Design, by
leaving out the Attick Story'. This meant
the reduction of the house from four to
three storeys, a new system of roofing, and
the contraction of the interior by nearly a
quarter.

No plans in Adam's hand appear to
survive nor any for these alterations apart
from a small drawing in the Blair Adam
collection. It shows a building smaller than
Duff House but with the same basic plan of
a square with four corner towers and
having the principal staircase in the same
position. There is another, similar drawing
at Cliveden in Berkshire which is fairly
close to the Blair Adam plan in both
composition and date. But if either of these
drawings had any bearing on the ultimate
plan for Duff House, it was only at a very
early stage and certainly not later than
1735. For in 1737, with the masons working
at cornice level, Lord Braco was still
uncertain of his mind. 'After I think hard
and forward on it,' he wrote to Adam in
May, 'I believe I'll not get over the Attick
Story, because the want of it would spoil
the looks of such a monstrous House'.
Presumably, both Adam and he now
returned to and continued with the original
scheme of 1735.

In 1739 the vexed attic storey had been

The *Generall Front of* DUFF HOUSE *toward the* Sea

The plans and elevation of Duff House in William Adam's Vitruvius Scoticus, *published in 1735. Although the house was designed with two wings, these were never built. A single wing to a different design was eventually added in 1870.* (Reproduced by kind permission of the Royal Commission on the Ancient and Historical Monuments of Scotland)

the Right Honerable the EARL of FIFE in the County of Banff.

Extends 230 feet.

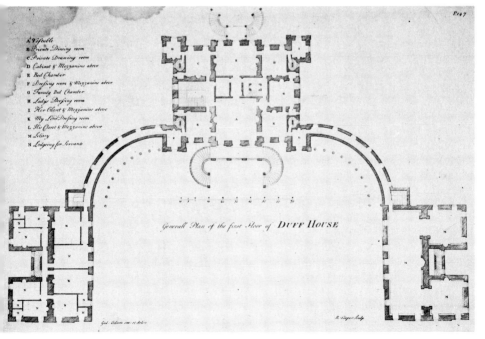

A Vestible
B Private Dining room
C Private Drawing room
D Cabinet & Mezzanino above
E Bed Chamber
F Dressing room & Mezzanine above
G Family Bed Chamber
H Ladys Dressing room
I Her Closet & Mezzanino above
K My Lords Dressing room
L His Closet & Mezzanino above
M Library
N Lodging for Servants

Pl. 47

Generall Plan of the first Floor of DUFF HOUSE

Gul. Adam inv. et delin.

R. Cooper Sculp.

9

built and work was in hand on the sculpture for the great pediment and on the statues, vases and balustrading that were to enliven the silhouette of the building. Here Adam was given by Lord Braco a sort of hesitant *carte blanche:* 'to make any little Alteration to the better as it occurred; and as happened in the last Year, with Respect to the Ballusters on the South Front, and the large windows for the great stair, on the West End'. In this way, Adam decided that the difficult and skilled carving of the various Corinthian and Composite capitals as well as the vases, coats of arms, and keystones, should not be done on the spot by the carving mason George Jamieson, but should be carried out in William Adam's yard at Queensferry and sent up in wooden crates to Banff by sea. By this arrangement John Burn carved at Queensferry twenty Corinthian and sixteen Composite capitals, thirty-four vases, two coats of arms, and six keystones, all of which were then separately boxed and sent to Banff at the total cost of approximately £2500 sterling. This was a large bill in eighteenth century

Four of the lead figures which adorned the pediments on the two principal fronts of Duff. These represent Minerva, Mars, Diana and Orpheus.

terms, and too large for Lord Braco to swallow. Work stopped on the house, and in 1741 there was a meeting of the lawyers on both sides to find a way out of the impasse. It failed, and the long, legal tangle that stretched from 1743 to 1748 began.

Legal Wrangles

William Adam's changing relations with Lord Braco are best seen through the law-suits whose source lay in the casual and ambiguous way both men had treated so important a commission. More surprising perhaps for Lord Braco, for he was an eminent man of affairs, much of whose success came from an able manipulation of the law and lawyers. It might unfairly be suggested that Lord Braco would not have undertaken such an operation if he had not shrewdly scented in such ambiguity a bargain within his grasp. The reverse was true of Adam, who was temperamentally

eless in money affairs—a trait apparent
his more famous son Robert. The Braco
e cannot have done him much
ofessional good. So little so, that at least
e intending client had to be reassured on
lam's character, 'he is far from being a
oney catcher; on the contrary he is very
en hit by the bargains he makes'. The
v-suit with Lord Braco lasted for five
ars, being settled shortly before William
lam's death in 1748. Both men felt
onged, and held that its shadow had
ghted at least part of their lives. In
lam's case it was true enough, for the
rmoil and anxiety of the case
doubtedly killed him.

The case was succinctly given in a
tition of November 1743. There Adam
as described as sueing Lord Braco 'for
yment of a considerable sum upon
ccount of a magnificent Family-seat built
r his Lordship; the Terms of the Bargain
ving been disputed, particularly whether
ur Petitioner (William Adam) was
ndertaker of the Building, or if his
ordship (Braco) himself was the
ndertaker'. Both claimed, according to
eir different systems, to have provided
en and material for Duff House and to
ave paid them. So much so, that Lord
raco inferred that if he now settled
dam's full claim he would have built Duff
louse twice over. Adam for his part
eclared he had made plans for both Duff
louse and the House of Airlie (Lord
raco's temporary home in Banff), built the
ansion house, and 'furnished several
onsiderable quantities of stone, timber,
ails, glass, and other materials', as well as
employed and paid out considerable sums
f Money to Artificers and workmen'. His
otal bill for all this was £9656, out of which
e gave Lord Braco credit for £3936, leaving
utstanding £5720. Of this, £2500 was
epresented by the various carved work
one in Adam's yard at Queensferry and
hipped up to Banff. Braco did not
hallenge this, but claimed that he had
een overcharged, understanding it would

*One of the Corinthian capitals made at Queensferry by
John Burn.*

cost no more, and be of better quality, if it
were done at Queensferry rather than
Banff. Nor did Lord Braco dispute in
principle that he owed Adam £363 for his
plans for Duff House, its mausoleum, and
temple, though he argued that he had paid
Adam between £30 and £55 per visit and
assumed these 'gratuities' sufficient. He
now added that he 'was never unwilling to
give him whatever might be thought a full
regard for his Labour and Trouble'.

After further delays, Petitions and a
general paralysis following the '45
rebellion, the case was finally settled in
April 1748. Under a judicial submission of
the law-lord Fletcher of Saltoun it was
found 'that after deduction of all payments
made by the said William Lord Braco or
other in his name that £2576 Sterling was
awarded to William Adam', a first
instalment of £500 falling due at Whitsun.
Sadly, it did Adam little good, for he died
in June and the balance was paid to John

The private dining room on the first floor, after restoration.

Adam in November of that year.

Obviously, little could be done to the house before the settlement of 1748 and by that time Lord Braco had lost both interest and heart. Certainly, when the Duke of Cumberland and the Hanoverian army appeared in Banff in 1745–46, he was entertained by Lord Braco at the House of Airlie, 'Duff House being', it was said, 'in an unfinished state, and without furniture'. He preferred to live at Balvenie and left the abandoned shell of Duff House to his son James, the future 2nd Earl Fife.

The 2nd Earl

When work came to an end in 1741, the building had been left incomplete and undecorated with the east and west colonnades, and the flanking pavilions not begun. But between 1748 and 1759, when an inventory of the house was made, most of the rooms on the ground floor and the first two floors had been fitted up, presumably for the use of Lord Macduff, the courtesy title for the future 2nd Earl Fife, and his wife. This inventory also showed that the vexatious attic storey was still unused, probably unfurnished and certainly without the library. Similarly incomplete were William Adam's two grand rooms of the salon and drawing room on the second floor (see the plan of that floor in about 1760 on page 20). In the furnished ground floor were all the servants under the eye of the steward and the housekeeper. On the first floor, that is

turned instead to the minor Irish architect John Woolfe in a belated attempt to add the missing wings to the house. In the end nothing came of the scheme for 'additions', except what is shown in Woolfe and Gandon's *Vitruvius Britannicus* of 1771 and Lord Fife's subscription to the volume.

The plate in *Vitruvius Britannicus* showed William Adam's pavilions and colonnades reworked in a more severe and neo-classic style, strongly horizontal, and more than a little at loggerheads with the baroque verticality of Adam's building. Woolfe's plan also suggested certain changes in the rooms since the 1759 Inventory. The most notable was the bringing of the salon from the second to the first floor where it took the place of the vestibule hall. The new wings were to contain principally the library in one, and a billiard room in the other. But perhaps the most distinct development, and one certainly after the 2nd Lord Fife's heart, was that the linking corridor from house to library pavilion was earmarked as a gallery for Lord Fife's burgeoning collection of historical portraits. The failure of these wings to materialise, though architecturally a blessing, left Duff House by both eighteenth and nineteenth century standards short of bedroom accommodation. It was a problem only resolved almost a hundred years later in 1870.

Though Lord Fife failed to finish the exterior of Duff, he successfully gave the house its impressive interior. In all of this he seems to have learnt from his father's experience and used both his own craftsmen and materials as well as dispensing with an architect. He appears to have acted as designer himself, certainly so in planning the lodges and eagle gates at the Banff Bridge entrance to the park in the 1770s. He was well served here and elsewhere on the estate by James Robertson the mason, and by his clerk of works Mr Dott. It was Dott who supervised all things at Duff House, personally taking charge of the gilding of the picture frames for Lord

he entrance storey, were the drawing and dining rooms with the remainder of the apartments divided between Lord and Lady Macduff. Above them on the second floor was a series of bedrooms one of which was used by Lady Fife and the rest named prosaically after the colour of their curtains—'Blew Damask, Green Gamblet, Blew Check, Sewed'.

The 1760s marked a determined effort by Lord Macduff, who succeeded his father as 2nd Earl in 1763, to finish the house and furnish it as grandly as possible. He was well cast for the role, pompous, authoritative with a strong sense of history, and an efficient administrator, with an interest in the arts and travel. In all of his architectural activities at Duff House he studiously avoided the Adam family, and

The pediment over the main entrance bearing the Duff arms and motto.

Fife's historical portraits, no mean task for a collection of nearly 286 works.

Yet for all Lord Fife's enthusiasm, work at Duff House proceeded slowly, possibly limited, as he claimed, by the expenses of his London home, Fife House, in Whitehall. In 1769, plasterwork was being carried out in the staircase hall by William Lyon, but surprisingly enough the staircase itself was either designed or redesigned by Lord Fife in 1791. Here again he was his own architect, paying Robertson £154 for thirty-five stone steps and the marble pavement at its foot. Fitting up the unfurnished rooms on the principal floor proceeded with equal caution and only in 1788 was one of the south-west bedrooms and its closet finished by the estate joiner Alexander Sangster. The attic storey, however, had been completed by 1776, for in that year the bulk of the library was removed from Rothiemay—another Fife property—to its new rooftop home.

At some time towards the end of the century a small building, a wash-house, white walled with a red tile roof, was incongruously attached to the east of the house. This wash-house wing may well have vanished only in 1870 when David Bryce junior, nephew of the more renowned David Bryce, replaced it with a corridor block and three storied pavilion in a solidly classical interpretation of William Adam's style. This provided the additional bedroom accommodation and also incorporated a billiard room without which no Victorian country house was complete. It was badly damaged by a stray bomb in 1941.

Duff in the Nineteenth Century

The 2nd Earl Fife died in 1809 and was succeeded by his brother Alexander who was followed in rapid succession by his son James as 4th Earl in 1811. The 4th Earl did not live at Duff House in any permanent way until around 1833. He seems to have preferred, possibly out of economy, the smaller scale of Delgatie Castle which had been bought in 1798. All of this was a far cry from the almost feudal splendour of Lord Braco and his son at Duff House, and reflected the extraordinary financial situation that prevailed after his uncle's will of 1809 and an earlier trust deed of 1801.

…e Banff bridge and the lodges on the main approach to Duff from the eastern side of the River Deveron. What is now the …ain road into Banff used to be the drive to Duff House; the main road itself used to swing sharply to the north to skirt the …ge of the park. The twin lodges which guarded this approach to the house are clearly visible in this view, but the southern of …e two was demolished to allow construction of a road of sufficient width.

…he Collie Lodge, which originally faced the northern approach to Duff from Banff. This elegant lodge, designed in the form of a …oric temple, is now the Tourist Information Office, and overlooks a public car park. In the distance the Temple of Venus may …e seen on the hilltop, where it formed a prominent eye-catcher from the park.

The future Edward vii *is entertained at Duff House in 1883. Large country houses like Duff only came alive during house parties such as this one: for much of the year the family resided elsewhere.* (Reproduced by kind permission of A J G Bodie, Banff)

The public face of Duff House: an amenities bazaar in the grounds in 1907. (Reproduced by kind permission of A J G Bodie, Banff)

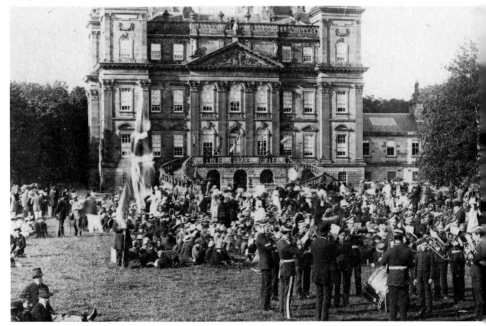

The history of Duff House in the twentieth century has been varied. Between 1911 and 1928 it was used as an hotel and sanatorium, before being requisitioned by the War Office in 1939. During the Second World War it served as a Prison of War for German Merchant Navy Officers, during which time the wing, built in 1870 (above), was badly damaged by a bomb. In the later war years the house was used as a billet for Norwegian and Polish troops, and for the King's Own Scottish Borderers. (Reproduced by kind permission of A J G Bodie, Banff)

According to the latter, the 2nd Earl Fife's illegitimate son enjoyed for life the Fife houses of Rothiemay, Innes, Delgatie, and Mar Lodge, with the remainder of the Fife estates severely entailed. All this led to a series of legal actions before the Court of Session and some of the property, notably Delgatie and Rothiemay, was recovered. But it left the Earldom both restricted and impoverished.

The 4th Earl was not a particularly frugal man, and his friendship with the Prince Regent, his taste for court life, and expensive electioneering in Elgin, did little to help a rickety financial situation, which was summed up in a sale at Duff House in 1824. Part of the Fife family silver was disposed of for £487, a certain amount of the furniture and 120 pictures and miniatures. The preamble to the sale catalogue itself bluntly stated that it was held 'on a warrant of the Sheriff of Banffshire for the payment of taxes'.

In 1875 the restraining entail on the Fife estates was broken. It coincided with the beginning of the agricultural depression which led to the break up of several very large Scottish estates. Fife was no exception. Sales had begun in the 1860s with the loss of Delgatie in 1863, the demolition sale of Fife House in London in 1869, and those of Rothiemay and Innes a few years later. Yet, despite both the decline in land values and shrinking acreage, the Fife estates stood at 257,657 acres in 1879 with an annual rental of £78,000. But the writing was on the wall, and, with the accession of the 6th Earl (and later 1st Duke) of Fife in 1879, its days were numbered. It was rarely used, and in 1906 the house and 140 acres of the park were presented jointly to Banff and Macduff, the pictures and contents consigned to the saleroom in 1907 and the gates closed on Lord Braco's descendants.

Its subsequent history as a hotel, nursing-home and army-billet was as chequered as it was unsuitable. Its acquisition by the Ministry of Works in 1956 was rescue at the eleventh hour, for by then Duff House was war-damaged and vandalised.

The vestibule in use as a drawing room in the late decades of the nineteenth century. The decoration of the walls and ceiling has recently been restored to the state shown here, although the rich profusion of furnishings and paintings is beyond recall.

THE FIFES AT HOME

or many the internal composition of a large eighteenth century house is something of a mystery. But it is a eful exercise to try to understand its ɟic, since the formality of society at that ne, with its emphasis on the public rather an private face and its often case-bound nventions, found fullest expression in the untry house. Its rooms all had a distinct le to play in this carefully graded society, d Duff House was no exception. Though e house has lost virtually all its original rnishings, it is still possible to reconstruct e purpose of each room and how it volved through the eighteenth and neteenth centuries. To this end the plates om William Adam's *Vitruvius Scoticus*, of 735, are of the greatest importance; these re complemented by an inventory of 1759, plan of 1771 in *Vitruvius Britannicus* and a icture catalogue of 1798. The way in which e house functioned in the nineteenth entury is glimpsed in the Sale Catalogue of 824, and in part by David Bryce junior's lans of 1870.

he Original Arrangements

'he progression and use of rooms intended y William Adam for Duff House in 1735 vas found only in his grandest houses. The pread of the principal public rooms over wo floors was unusual in this period, specially in Scotland, and its effect was to ;ive Duff House a particular spatial ;randeur. The vestibule on the first floor pened off the main entrance to the house, nd allowed waiting space for important ;uests: it was reached by an imposing xternal horseshoe stair. But those visitors

of lesser rank, and those on estate business were expected to use side doors on the ground floor, or the entrance below the horseshoe stair. The vestibule was effectively isolated from the family rooms which occupied much of the rest of the first floor, although relatively easy access was provided to the room intended as Lord Fife's dressing room, where much of the day-to-day administration of the estate was discussed.

To the north of the vestibule were the private drawing and dining rooms, whilst the rooms to the east were designed as a family apartment, with two large dressing rooms opening out of a family bedroom. The dressing rooms were ingeniously linked vertically to similar rooms at an intermediate level above by oval backstairs which, in medieval fashion, were hidden in the thickness of the walls. They provided the servants with ready access to the principal bedrooms, and allowed them to fetch and carry promptly—and virtually unseen.

The nurseries were to have been on the floor below, and were linked to the family apartment by the spiral backstairs. Elsewhere on the ground floor were the more menial rooms necessary for a great country house, such as the housekeeper's quarters, the servants' hall, pantry, wine and ale cellars. The humbler rooms, like milk houses, laundries, and servants' rooms were to have been consigned to the two pavilions, while the kitchen was to have been located in the centre of a nest of ancillary rooms in the west pavilion. The failure to build the pavilions inevitably

19

FIRST FLOOR ABOUT 1760

DRAWING ROOM

DINING ROOM

LADY MACDUFF'S DRESSING ROOM

STAIRS

LADY MACDUFF'S BEDROOM

VESTIBULE

LORD MACDUFF'S DRESSING ROOM

N

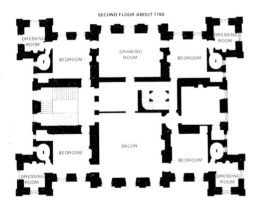

SECOND FLOOR ABOUT 1760

DRESSING ROOM

BEDROOM

DRAWING ROOM

BEDROOM

DRESSING ROOM

BEDROOM

SALON

BEDROOM

DRESSING ROOM

DRESSING ROOM

element for many years. Culminating the public parade through the house and at the head of the stair, were the salon and great drawing room on the central axis of the second floor. Disposed around these, at the four corners of the house, were spacious guest apartments each consisting of a bed and dressing room, with a servant's room above the latter. Adam intended that the attic storey, which could be reached only by the lesser staircases, should be divided between a gallery running the length of the west side of the house, and a series of secondary bedrooms. The former was planned as a rectangular room, sixty feet long, intended to contain pictures and other works of art and also to provide a form of indoor exercise room in the tradition of the renaissance Long Gallery.

The 2nd Earl

By the time of the inventory of 1759, Duff House had been reorganised for Lord Macduff, the future 2nd Lord Fife, both to function without wings, and to house a child-less family of estranged husband and wife. It was too a house where the principal staircase and at least two of its grandest rooms, the salon and drawing room were incomplete, although the second floor bedrooms were more or less finished. One of them was being used in 1759 by Lady Fife, the mother of the 2nd Earl, who died in 1788. Communication between this and the first floor must have been awkward, since the main staircase was only completed in 1791. The back and spiral stairs had to serve in its place, and this probably encouraged the use of the eastern side of the house.

On the first floor the vestibule, private drawing room and private dining room were used according to Adam's intentions, but Adam's ill-fated family bedroom had become that of Lady Macduff, with the adjoining room as her dressing room. Her husband used the related room at the south-east corner as his dressing room, but he seems to have occupied a bedroom

meant that Duff House was chronically short of such accommodation virtually throughout its history.

The link between the first floor entrance and the major public rooms on the second floor was always intended to be the main staircase, although the untimely abandonment of the first building operation was to leave the house without this

ove it on the second floor. Such an
angement kept his wife's room at an
derstandable distance whilst the
proprieties of the family wing were
perficially maintained. Other changes of
action took place on the attic floor in the
sence of the intended pavilions: in the
llery the 2nd Lord Fife finally set up his
her's library, and his own collection of
ins and antiquities.

More radical changes are suggested in
oolfe's unexecuted designs of 1771 for the
dition of wings, although caution is
cessary since he may have been showing
proposed rather than existing interior
rangement. Certainly, he revealed no
w structural changes, and his most
gnificant suggestion was to bring the
lon down from the second to the first
oor, with a corresponding dispatch of the
ivate drawing room upstairs. The
ojected revival of the wings was to have
cluded a long picture gallery, culminating
a new library in the west pavilion. By
ontrast the east pavilion would have been
intellectual anticlimax, having a billiard
om as its principal chamber.

uff House in the Nineteenth Century

good insight into life at Duff House on
he eve of the nineteenth century is given
y the names of the various rooms in Lord
ife's catalogue of his picture collection of
798. According to it Woolfe's salon had
everted to a vestibule though the adjoining
arge room on the north front remained as
he dining room, and his breakfast room in
he south-east corner had become a
arlour. The drawing room stayed where
Adam had fixed it in 1735, but the cabinet
n the south-west corner had become a blue
drawing room. At the top of the newly
ompleted grand staircase, the former salon
vas now the large drawing room with
cross the corridor Adam's great drawing
oom, now termed the north drawing
oom. In fact Duff House had in 1798 three
uch rooms. This pattern remained until
824 at least, when the rooms were again

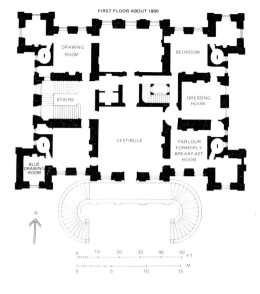

The vestibule as recently restored. The trompe e'oeuil
*decoration of the dado and the palmette border to the walls
were found beneath hotel period decoration, and have been
carefully restored to their later nineteenth century state.
The ceiling, chimney piece and doorcases are still in their
eighteenth century form.*

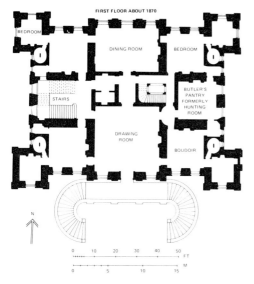

described in some detail in the Sale Catalogue of 1824. According to its room room description, William Adam's ill-fated family bedroom, later Lady Fife's, had now become the 'Hunting Room', fitted up rather strangely with 'An elegant Mahogany French Bed . . . said to have formerly belonged to Napoleon Buonaparte', and no doubt part of the 4th Earl's Peninsular War booty. Lord Fife's bedroom and dressing room were now upstairs at the north-west corner, next door to the north drawing room. As the 4th Earl was in 1824 both a bachelor and set in his ways, Duff House was unlikely to have changed much until his death in 1857.

In 1870, and at long last, the 5th Earl built a single wing and pavilion to the east of the Adam house after the design of David

The drawing room about 1890. (Reproduced by kind permission of A J G Bodie, Banff)

ce junior. His plan for this addition
unately showed not only the proposed
v rooms but the disposition of the
sting rooms on the entrance floor. The
ing room remained as in Adam's plan,
the parlour had undergone a further
nsformation into boudoir, the 'Hunting
om' of 1824 had now been divided into a
ler's pantry and part of a passage-way
ding to the new wing. Apart from these
anges, this floor of the house had
ome increasingly domestic and less
nd with the blue drawing room of 1798
ned into a bedroom. The new wing itself
atained seven more bedrooms and a
iard room.

After such a rearrangement, the great
ne of musical rooms at Duff House came
an end in 1870. Little happened of any

consequence until the building ceased to be
a private home in 1903. After that furniture
and pictures were dispersed so completely
that Duff House lost all but its architectural
meaning. The rooms themselves that had
moved so well to the changing music of
their times at last rested.

*The saloon in its early twentieth century state when in use
as a hotel. The potted palms and basket chairs are
characteristic of the type of furnishings to be found in the
better hotels of the period.*

THE PARK

An essential part of any country house was its surrounding parkland. It gave a controlled setting for the building and provided a series of prospects from the windows of the house. It reflected in miniature the crucial relationship between landlord and tenant and symbolically expressed an ideal which in the case of Duff House was one where 'Opression, discord, found no place; Art, Science, Equity and Love are seen'. The park at Duff House was essentially the creation of the 2nd Earl Fife which, like the house itself, was left to mature largely undisturbed throughout the nineteenth century.

The first scheme for forming an ornamental park at Duff House was made by William Adam in 1735. In October, Lord Braco wrote to William Adam that 'I shall be glad you make out the Plan of my Garden conform to the Lines you took; and though it will be some Time before I can put anything in Execution as to that, yet I wish to have it in my View to do it in the best Manner. Boutcher was lately in this Country, I have likewise put it on him to make out a plan of my Ground, I want to glean from all Quarters in this Matter, and keep by what is best'. Neither Adam's design nor those of William Boutcher, the nursery-man from Comely Bank in Edinburgh, have survived.

A late eighteenth century watercolour of Duff House and park by Thomas Girtin. (Reproduced by kind permission of the Ashmolean Museum, Oxford)

The Island Temple, now ruinous, stands on the banks of the River Deveron and was built after the design of William Adam.
(Reproduced by kind permission of the Royal Commission on the Ancient and Historical Monuments of Scotland)

According to William Adam's *State of Process* of 1743, his plan for the park was never carried out, but the Temple he designed for 'an island of the River Divern . . . was accordingly built'. This survives though now in a ruinous condition. Known as the fishing pavilion, it is a small circular structure with a pedimented entrance built without decoration in stone. Whatever its visual function in Adam's scheme for the park, in the 1760s it marked the end of the riverside walk coming down-stream from the Bridge of Alvah. This walk along the banks of the Deveron was of considerable importance. Carried out in 1767, it marked a significant change of taste, a substitution of the mainly formal design of William Adam for one which was much more natural and closer to the ideals of the landscape garden.

A sheet of drawings for a pavilion, walled garden, and farm house by William Bowie probably point to his being the designer of this phase of the landscape at Duff. Bowie enjoyed a reputation in the

1750s as a gardener in the 'natural way' and had a considerable practice in Edinburgh and the Lothians as well as in the North of England. It is likely that it was Bowie's ideas that Lord Fife's gardener, Thomas Reid, was carrying out when he wrote to the 2nd Earl reporting planting in most places at Duff House and the forming of 'a small walk made along the waterside which is near finished from the Bridge at Banff to the Bridge at Alvah'. It was this walk that later connected the various garden buildings—the mausoleum, the mount and the Gothic tower at the Bridge of Alvah, and was paralleled on higher ground with the carriage way to Duff House from Montcoffer and the west. Some idea of how it looked in its heyday is given in the brilliant gouache of Charles Cordiner's which shows Lord Fife's coach and six crossing the Bridge of Alvah, rebuilt in 1772, to begin their descent to Duff House through this enchanted riparian landscape.

The other side of the gardening coin in the eighteenth century was the walled

painting, 'The Bridge of Alvah, Duff House' by Charles Cordiner. (Private Collection)

rden, which gratified the more prosaic eds of a great country house. That of uff House survives, though cut off from e park by a new road which ironically llows the line of that originally moved stwards by Lord Braco in 1735. In 1767, eid wrote that the fruit trees from France d come and that 'some days ago I have anted ten of the Pears on the Brick wall to and with some of the Peaches and pricot. The rest is put in Betwixt the trees the wall, to preserve them until the arden wall be Built, the Apples and Some the pears in the Nursery. They were ceedingly Dry having no Moss or any ing but Straw put about their roots . . . e Roses is all safe being packed with loss. I think the French Gardener bad acker of trees and no better Marker of em. The small Rolls of pepr with their ames was so rotten that Sundries of them uld not be known.'

In 1791, the 2nd Earl Fife then aged 62 egan to consider building a mausoleum either in the park at Duff House or in the new town at Macduff. In this he was renewing his father's idea, for William Adam had listed a design for a mausoleum in the *State of Process* of 1743. Lord Fife settled for the park and used the site of a former Convent of the Carmelites, and to emphasise the antiquity of the new structure decorated the exterior in the old-fashioned style of the Rococo Gothic. Lord Fife then began a rather undignified hunt for ancestors with whom to give some sense of tradition and continuity to the new mausoleum. He took sculptured monuments from the churches at both Banff and Cullen and these were set up and adapted to correspond to the paternal monument he had erected in the mausoleum in 1792.

According to J C Loudon's *Encyclopaedia of Gardening* of 1822, the park was modernised probably some time in the 1780s. The landscape gardener for this last phase of the development of the garden was

The remains of the mausoleum built by the 2nd Earl Fife on the site of a Carmelite chapel. (Reproduced by kind permission of A J G Bodie, Banff)

Thomas White, a Nottinghamshire designer with an important practice in the North of England and an extensive one in Scotland. He was at Gordon Castle, in 1786, and at Cullen House in 1789, and probably worked at Duff House between these dates. White was a highly competent if rather unimaginative designer in the Capability Brown tradition. Regrettably his suggested improvement plan has not survived. But the final shape taken by the grounds around the house and the Deveron, where the park included four parishes, was White's interpretation of the great set pieces of the eighteenth century landscape movement.

The park at Duff House was an important one. Though the combination of scattered trees and a smooth lawn around the house was unremarkable, even unimaginative, the riverside walk of the 1760s and the carriageway from the Bridge of Alvah were both outstanding in their exploitation of the natural landscape. While this great park played several roles—model farm, experimental woodland, and game preserve, its essential character was that of an idealised landscape, a sort of Garden of Eden, where landlord, tenant, and employee lived at peace, hopefully.

Acknowledgements
Professor Tait is greatly indebted to Capt. Ramsay of Mar for access to the Montcoffer (Fife) Papers and to Mr. John Bates of the Scottish Record Office.